Volume 84

of the

Yale Series

of Younger

Poets

Out
of
the
Woods

Thomas Bolt

Foreword by James Merrill

Yale University Press

New Haven & London

Publication of this volume was made possible
by a gift from The Guinzburg Fund.

Set in Ehrhardt type by
Tseng Information Systems.
Printed in the United States of America.

Library of Congress
Cataloging-in-Publication Data
Bolt, Thomas, 1959–
    Out of the woods / Thomas Bolt; foreword by
    James Merrill. p.   cm.—(Yale series of
    younger poets; v. 84)
    ISBN 0–300–04469–0 (alk. paper).—ISBN
    0–300–04468–2 (pbk.: alk. paper)
    I. Title.   II. Series.
    PS3552.05875098   1989
    811'.54—dc 19   88–30313
                              CIP

The paper in this book meets the guidelines for
permanence and durability of the Committee on
Production Guidelines for Book Longevity of the
Council on Library Resources.
10 9 8 7 6 5 4 3 2 1

for

Renée Bucciarelli

and for Cary

Contents

Foreword

As we know from galleries hung with studies of the same apple-strewn tablecloth, the painter who mines a single vein is felt to have looked profoundly into both his subject and himself. But for a poet to dwell, page after page, upon the same small family of images may argue a certain limitation. Language is after all an Ariel free, unlike the Calibans of brush and pigment, to embody every nameable bit of the universe. Here, though, is Thomas Bolt, whose grimy, late twentieth-century pastoral fills up a whole book. Has motif given way to obsession? The corner Bolt paints himself into commands too wide and too sobering a view for us to think so.

The scene could be almost anywhere in the original thirteen colonies. It is largely unpeopled, but not idyllically so. Human-kind is very much present in the things it has used and discarded. We recognize all too well those wrecked cars, rusted appliances, empty Clorox bottles. Like the soil itself they represent our common heritage, having merged by now with the abandoned orchard and picturesquely decaying homestead that horrify the visitor from abroad. Good land neglected—what madness! No wonder America produces children it then ignores, who will grow up to be killers. No wonder its principal exports in 1986 were scrap metal and waste paper. Such facts positively quiver to fuel a fire-and-brimstone sermon. Bolt, however, remains cool, sharply focused; a steady hand crops his lines. Not to worry, he might be telling us: the worst is over. Apocalypse has already taken place, long ago, at some remote juncture in our lives. The evidence lies all around us.

Fortunately there are overtones that sweeten the pill. Just as the famous red wheelbarrow surrounded by chickens merges—in the mind of a reader given to association—with Aphrodite's sparrow-drawn chariot, so the woods in which Bolt keeps losing and finding himself tend to be more than mere doomed sylvan interstices in our urban sprawl. They come to him by way of

Dante and Auden, Augustine and Thoreau. Centuries ago he
might have written:

> Already my slow steps had carried me
> Into the ancient wood so far, that I
> Could not perceive where I had entered it.
> And lo! my further course a stream cut off. . . .
> (*Purgatorio* XXVIII, trans. Longfellow)

Instead:

> I shook from my own shudder of surfaces
> And heard the sound
> Of the narrow water, moving as before
> Between where I was
> And had to go; I balanced at the edge,
> And crossed the creek.

Writing a poem, or reading one, is always to some degree
a spiritual exercise. A reader who, understandably nowadays,
wants to skip the allegory, still responds to Dante's urgent topog-
raphy, and it is a kindred energy in Bolt that keeps us on his
track. Whatever his woods once "stood for"—sin, unredeemed
human nature, the animistic emperies of Pan—he can't be much
bothered to recall. Oh, here and there an old Pontiac suggests
"truth / . . . up on cinderblocks," and a "barren ditch" turns into
"the ditch of belief." Yet considering how prodigally another poet
might have strewn his way out of the woods with italicized Hindu
or Christian terminology, we can overlook a few youthful indul-
gences. More to the point, by sidestepping the overtly personal,
Bolt shows not alienation but good sense. As in that parlor game
beloved by amateur psychologists, the subject who describes the
elements of a made-up landscape—the key underfoot, the body
of water, the old wall—has already revealed himself with respect
to religion, Eros, and death. Here the entire metaphorical field

is so rich that the plainest words—path, tie, lot, dark, flow—
vibrate from the start with human overtones.

Bolt's fullest investigation of his dark wood takes up the last
half of his book—a single poem. Partly followed, partly impro-
vised, its path is too arduous for the imagination to stray very far.
There are no "flights," just the syntactical coping with a terrain
brought line by line onto the page. The one backward look in
time (late in section I) is rendered in images of the here and now.
Accordingly the reader must bear some of the protagonist's frus-
trations. But the adventure is so vivid, so psychologically engag-
ing—as it moves from thicket to railroad track, from swamp to
"good, cold creek cleaning its bed / Of mattress-springs," from
field strewn with "great, annihilated iron things" to a vast junk-
yard where Dante, as it were, meets Henry Ford and which Bolt's
exertions earn him the momentary right to claim as "The secret
center of America"—that we too are left with second wind and
want nothing more than to read the poem all over again.

On so doing, many lovely progressions and adjustments will
come to light. A single illustration. In section II "tall sycamores /
Still hung with burrs" appear. In III the sky, seen through "skin
and bones of tattered sycamores," is "Nailed to naked branches
overhead / With iron burrs." Later (VI) come "decorated syca-
mores, / Bone white, / Hung with round burrs / Like orna-
ments." And finally, "starry points of sycamore burrs / . . .
buried / In the smoke of the cold sky darkening." These varia-
tions have a concise logic. The burrs, first nailheads as of a
crucifixion, then ornaments as on a Christmas tree, sparkle forth
from murk at the close, a humble *cielo stellato* to welcome the
fulfilled pilgrim.

In "Temporary Structure" Bolt returns to an earlier image:
a bucket slowly disintegrating in the creek where "it is beaten
back and forth." It is the form given by thought and language to
a present continually improvised,

New, a booming shape
Banged and battered,
Its drum curve
Beaten by water,
Its flattened crystals blazing
Jammed between rocks,
One side in silver shadow.

. . . .

Turned and overturned,
Bright zinc will wear off,

The bottom pock with rust,
Each pock
Enlarge with ruin, and,
Worn to a wafer,
The whole, punctured crust
Finally crumple under a loop
Of new water into a whorl of flakes.

Now charged by electrical alliterations, now at rest in a random pentameter, the language lightly thuds and dances; the *k* and *b* sounds of *bucket* ricochet, dispersing within its description like bits of the thing itself. If, presently, we pause to notice how "whole" relates to "punctured," or "wafer" to "crust," or if Bolt himself pauses long enough to reflect that

This living framework,
Scaffold for a life,
Will plunge into a cold scattering

. . . .

The scaffolding of my language taken down
Leave an emptiness of objects,

it may seem that simple justice has been done to incoherent nature's way with words.

James Merrill

Acknowledgments

"Meditation in Loudoun County" and "Unauthorized Dump" first appeared in *Southwest Review*. "1971 Pontiac LeMans" first appeared in *The Paris Review*.

"Thomas Eakins: Max Schmitt in a Single Scull" first appeared as section IV of a sequence entitled "American Art" in *Land*, a limited edition hand printed by the author (copyright © 1982 by Thomas Bolt).

Thanks to Margaret Bowland Harris for her detailed criticisms. Thanks also to A. H., G. O., and J. H. "The Ditch" is dedicated to Jack Beal.

Notes

The paintings referred to in "Thomas Eakins: Max Schmitt in a Single Scull" are: *Max Schmitt in a Single Scull*, 1871, oil on canvas, 32¼×46¼ inches, Metropolitan Museum of Art, New York; and *The Gross Clinic*, 1875, oil on canvas, 96×78 inches, Jefferson Medical College, Philadelphia.

The last two lines of "Spring Morning, 1952" are the words of Edward Teller, the principal inventor of the hydrogen bomb, quoted from a television interview with Larry King. Dr. Teller was explaining why he had never attended a test of the hydrogen bomb, which was first exploded in 1952. (Larry King and Emily Yoffe, *Larry King*, New York, Simon and Schuster, 1982, page 156.)

A Hill in Virginia

In this rude world
Memory pertains
In bald things,
Of promises skipped over, violence
Or accidents of kissing.
Read within the deep patina
Of the old stump
Of a chainsawed black walnut
Its circular
History from sex to ruin;

Look where
Cracked and spattered chunks
Of cold quartz
Stuck in mud
Glitter up from a dull hill.
Downhill, the wrecked car:
A punched-in windshield
Sags whole,
An afterimage of collision,
Brilliant with sky.

Unpolluted Creek

All day,
Iron flecks
Sprinkle from the shell
Of a galvanized bucket,
Its bottom gone,
The clean sides being slowly punctured.

If anything happens here
In the changing sun
Among weeds and stripped metals,
It is only water
Picking through junk, gradually
Enlarging flaws.

Also, among disconnected hoses
In the speckled back
Of a gutted dishwasher,
The smooth paint
Being furred with white mold;
There is no hurry.

What is not important here
Is not important.

The Ditch

I too was almost digested by the city:
All my purposes had ended there
But a few necessary simple ones.
I rose up;
Having no other choice,

Since even the road behind me
If I turned
Would stand ahead,
I went along the road for many miles
With the taste of the past in my mouth.

The stars came out,
The moon turned in,
And I endured the sun, the stars again,
The populated sky, the emptying
Of dusk over and over as I walked.

At last
I came to the place past failure
Where anyone can rest,
And slept a long time
To empty myself of dreams.

The last dream was this:
That I had come
For many miles along a barren ditch,
Past help or faith in help,
Where disappointment led me; to myself.

Morning was cool and hard.
I saw there was no road, nor had there been.
I stood in an enormous wilderness,
Blistered and dumb and empty, and I looked
On all the nothing I have ever known.

That was no place at all;
It had no boundaries, but was a kind
Of nothing between nothings, where I stood
Considering nothing;
Nothing mattered much;

Nothing fell like manna from the sky,
Nothing tempted me with stony loaves
And nothing struck a serpent from the sticks;
Nothing oppressed me; nothing let me go;
I could have lived on nothing all my life,

But I was low, and hungrier than that.
The day was hard and hot.
Because I had no choice,
I squatted there, and dug
In the ditch of belief.

After a Terrible Thing Happened

I emerged from that place
    Owning nothing
And came to this place where the path makes
    A rough mosaic
Out of the scattered gravels and busted jars,
    To find nothing more

Than what I saw wrecked black-barked in a jumble of vine,
    Its mud-spattered
Entanglement of branches strangling the creek,
    Its heart involved
In knotted roots nerved with a fine hair;
    So I walked awhile

After the intelligence at the hull of things
    Neglected not saved
And crusted with other lives than our own:
    Until I felt
My skeleton turn to old iron
    Forgotten in the mud

Edging a scrap-grounds. There were a few trees,
    Thin saplings,
Hard by a broader wood of sycamores
    Where no one looked.
My cold metals sank in the stunned-still world
    All day

As only shadows moved over the dirt
    And wreckage
And spidery nerves of root
    Where a tree
Caught between others leaned over the creek:
    All day

Sun burned on the unsalvaged metal
    And moved slowly away
Over the stubs of weeds at the woods' edge
    Until light eroded
Red in the distant emptiness of fields
    Where dismantled things

Sank in embedded mud. A loose tree propped alive
    Where only
A thicket of other limbs prevented its
    Tearing away
From the bank it held part-lifted in its roots,
    Leaned still

While the shadow of the woods crossed
    Fallen things
Strewn with broken glass, and a far scattering of nuts
    Cracked by the sun
Or rotten, bruised and buried: whatever there was stood
    While only the light moved

On my iron skeleton rusting in the mud.
    Those acorns cast
Shadows the length of oaks and the transparent
    Color of locust shells
Over the wilderness of abandoned chassis
    Where I stood

Watching the scrap-grounds darken in the shape
    Of the caught tree
Hung half-dangling; and its slow roots forgot
    The tangled shape
They had displaced for years in the packed bank,
    And felt for other mud.

My nerves felt for the world:
　　　All afternoon,
With the slow burn-out of daylight on the limbs,
　　　I watched
Things shift through the empty rungs of trees
　　　Until I felt myself

Lurched-loose and uprooted over the strangled creek
　　　And scrap of the world,
Restrained only in iron-gray tanglings;
　　　But I turned
From the shock of being torn away
　　　To move again.

I walked to the next place on a rough path
　　　Through the shifted woods
Where that ruined metal sank in the rusting sun
　　　All afternoon,
As its cast-off purpose blackened with other scrap
　　　Left unclaimed

In the taste of the mineral, November air,
　　　And its flawed ribs
Stuck from the weedless mud
　　　Dead-still by the brown
Water of the long ditch where the shadow fell,
　　　Wrecked and loosening

In the only world that happens.

Facing Southwest, June 14, 5:50 P.M.

Shadows lean to the left from a clump of pines,
Along the ridge of a bland hill. Closer up,
Rocks on the clay bank sweat in the cooling shadow
Of overhanging weeds. Light enters the few shrubs
From the right, reddish, filtering through a coolant
Of shovel-shaped leaves to emerge as bluish shade.
An odor of pines: branches relax and flex,
Grasses scissor and shuffle in a lull
Of water noises. The car keys jingle.

1971 Pontiac LeMans

Auto in sunlight: every trace of gloss
Is dulled a rusting green.
Even the fenders are a dirty chrome
Which blunts light like a pine log;
Still, it runs.

This is the car someone abandons
At a grassy roadside,
Like an old punt, rotten-hulled,
Sunk in river muck above the seats.
Near this realization,

It will do 90 still.
Or, filled with gasoline, will drive all night
Toward any destination;
It can kill.
This is the real world.

Six Descriptions

I

My mother kept the crippled owl
On a permit from the Fish and Wildlife Service;
Perched on our screen porch, it would hiss
And clack its beak when I left on an errand.
My mother in the kitchen killing sparrows
For the owl: too many of them
Preempt nuthatch and bluebird, so she cups
Each trapped friend in her palm, and takes its life
Between the thumb and fingers gently.

II

Exploring the cut of the stream:
Weeds curve green ribs over mud,
Shale parts in baking sun
Like the feathery sinuses
In the nose of a skull,
Watery ligaments grip the yellow rocks.
And, knowing the realness of the quartz,
The sun sure as a pebble,
I am happy here.

III

I opened the freezer door to get some ice:
Three rats dropped out,
Pink, frozen twists of meat
Bought from government labs to feed the owl.
I saw them later, thawing on the porch;
Then bloated and headless on his feeding-stump,
Pink-and-white plumpness of mortality.
He savors the head, skull fur and brains,
Disdains the bodies fat as the hands of an aunt.

IV

The first day at the beach I wakened early
And, walking, saw among alluvial scum,
On flat sand freckled with weed-bits,
The empty helmet of a horseshoe crab.
How could one so armored come to this?
The air came pure from over sea,
And the wakening morning,
Lapping its tides of dry light
Over the still, brown bowl.

V

After we viewed the body in its casket
My great-grandfather explained, outside,
How bricks, ground back into red dust,
Were part of the dirt we stepped on,
And houses, buried under deep layers,
Were forgotten and built upon; until I saw
Bones sprouting hard buds
In the graveyards, like potatoes left too long
In a dark kitchen cabinet.

VI

I was six. They lifted me up to see the uncle.
I could not tell what it was,
But knew the half-shown thing
Was not a man;
Digging, at eight, the cut of a root surprised me:
I drew back, tearless, staring at the deep
Loam-crammed wound beginning to bleed.
Inside, rinsing the cut under the tap,
I saw with wonder into my own flesh.

Meditation in Loudoun County

The Pontiac
Is a natural object. Ice melting on its hood
Trickles along a warp to the front end,
Drips from chromed fenders to the gravel
Making ticking sounds. Expanding metal,

Late spring.
Bloomed honeysuckle wavers in the chainlink,
Wilting. Still the car sits still: its metal,
Bled up through dulled enamel, rusts
In the hot sun of the front yard,

Throttled
By dried weeds. Punctures open into crusts.
Dead, flat enamels pucker into blisters.
Chromes flake and sprinkle gravel. A pale dust
Coats the hubcaps.

If truth
Is up on cinderblocks in the noon sun,
The color leaches from its dented door.
All day sun burns into the battered hood.
The earth is conservative. The car sits still.

Desire

Some change of body or some change of mind
Has cleared the world
I found
This morning, dried
Like an old sheet hung out in the sun.

I found a scorched past
Cooled of its smoke and spent.
The air tasted of it, but refreshed
And filtering;
Above, beyond the field fallen to char,

The necessary world was still alive.
The cracked and scattered woods
Wore fuel
Gathered from years of standing in the sun,
Rooted in tight channels of dirt;

To one side, almost leveled for new growth,
The junk was blackened back to element,
Though here and there, a magazine or tire
Smoldered
Flickering back toward value, to be lost.

Whatever the old life had been
Was a stain lifted on the oil of my thumb.
The day
Was stripped of squandered purposes,
And the gloss of vision buckled to what was there.

So I toured
This new, unwanted ground
Animals scavenged on,
Which soured with depletion and exhaust
Whenever the wind changed.

What I had survived
I saw a little of, but nothing more
Than a broken heel, the fragment of a glass,
The dirty water
Screwed to a drain.

The lost heat
Had withered me alive and made me lean,
As though I had, stripped naked in this field,
Been blistered to coarse essence
Until there was no defense or need of such.

My brain was in my skin.
Then over the damp ash
Moving air
Crossed the uneven stakes of abandoned plots,
Unraveling scraps of twine; and the wind

Ranged out and sifted through
The wide-open expanse of blackened grass
And wreck of motives,
Uncovering
What could not be consumed

To a day
All residue and freshness,
As if fire
Burned appetite away
And left desire.

Standing in a Clearing

What will you do, the large world
Scattered behind you, leaves a live red?
As dead branches crack under your feet
And you look across
The tilted face of a stump
At stories of orbit and eclipse
In a whorl of sawmarks,

What will you do?
In this inexpedient place,
Sun eats the heavy paint
From 55-gallon drums;
Your whirled nerves
Are worth no more than leaves, your fingernail
Is dead as the branch your foot lifts.

What will you do?
The pattern of past growth
Circles its axis of origin, hardening
In its own acids; but can still become
Whatever you want to make of every day
Of the long years
Stored in the pine stump like a battery.

Here, dialectic washes in the mud.
What, the world your wood,
Will you do with life
Explosive in the sun
In its chemical miracle,
Consumed as you are in this place,
In the moment of your hand

On the motor housing,
Fingering marks of dried gasoline?
Afoul of fall, the leaves
Are fouled with all, fluttering, falling,
Found underfoot,
A sound underfoot,
Rot under root,

Barked with the brown of days, done, down,
All ground and sand unsound underfoot;
And with your only life
Widening from a point
Of origin, and bound
By dark encircling crust, you stand
Almost autonomous,

Ringed by the fallen bronze
Of the trees
Which rise between down and none
And noun and done,
To choose whatever you can
If you can
As all the stained wood is dyed and dries.

These motley leaves
Are made the fools of fall;
Now that the air has made a fuel of all,
An unclogged ooze of days
Wrung from the trees,
A rotten ripeness looks from every pool.
Tasting fall in the fell cool of the wood, what

Are you going to do with your life?
After the caught
Noise, vibrant rasp, and rise
Of chainsaw sounds
You are
The gasoline motor shaking in your hands,
The smell of fuel,

The readiness of air.

Thomas Eakins:
Max Schmitt in a Single Scull

Eakins looks toward the vivid bridge,
The mechanism of his brush and eye
Surgical and objective as a lens.
The ochres of a Pennsylvania fall
Fuzz toward the sky, the moment's poise preserved
And justified. The second bridge is red,
Deciduous branches bare. Red maple leaves
Grip sapless limbs. Mud flattens toward the water
Slipping under. By the first bridge a canoe
Is red and holds three men; a second scull
Moves pocking water with the pull of oars,
Its slaps just fading. Mallards fuss and drift,
A scull mosquitos by the distant bank.
Schmitt drifts back in the vivisected day.

Glimpse of Terrain

One kind of logic is a road cut into the side of a steep, wooded hill.
Its engineering makes travel of several kinds possible.
The road describes itself
(From a train I saw the profile
Of road and hill, the hill without the road
Covered with trees and rocks,
With dirt and leaves and fossil histories,
And the road set out from plan, graded from point to point,
A doubled yellow line curving with it,
Its asphalt smooth and banked efficiently,
Following every degree of the built bed).
It does not describe the hill.

Creek near Leesburg

A refrigerator
Dumped in the creek,
With a frame of mattress-springs:
Rust crawls under white enamels
Like water opening under ice.

I look hard; I am a reporter
Of the unimportant:
That the whole woods is red,
The dullish colors of rust and dead lumber
Fallen into afternoon light.

I want to know
What is not news:
The creek flooding a narrow oven
Dumped from the bank upstream,
Wedged half-submerged and battered against rocks;

The rust crinkling under industrial paint,
The slowly rising water;
Whatever we cannot invent, being part of.
These things
Survive any commentary.

Unauthorized Dump

Where general sun breaks down
In specific weeds,
Iron is invaded by air:
A doorless dryer
Tilts open upward,
Half-full of muddy water
And blackening clumps of leaves.

Something's coming other than the spring.
Late afternoon moves like a bulldozer
Over surrounding hills
Abandoned to growth;
By the river, trees
Fallen into the embrace of mud
Sink and darken,

And still the bed's uncovered skeleton
Remembers no marriage:
Each helix of its wired cage of springs
Adapts to the pile of chunked cement and rock
Where it was dumped.
Where general sun breaks down
In a few million weeds,

Crossing a dead stream and running out
Into the littered shadow of the wood,
The Ideal loses impetus.
Yet something keeps: what is it? In the sky,
A fallen color? Blackness in the leaves
Of the final rust
Metal concedes to air?

Even here, in this zero place
With fallen things
Stripped of decoration,
Scattered out
Like acorns, hardware, bones, like anything,
Something resists subtraction,
And is left.

The living nerve,
In its supple duct of cartilage and bone,
Knows, besides the hill
Scattered with shade and seed,
The old frameworks sprawling in the dirt,
Or the rusty coils
Holding their skeleton shape against the rocks,

That something else is here.
Outside our ignorance and entertainment,
There is another order to the world:
It is that thing
Left in unanswered silence after movement.
There is no description for it.

It is here to stay.

Storage Shed

Gray and violet shingles on the pine.
Tulips vivid, unnatural. Clothesline,
Two sheds, one blossoming with rust
Through white enamel paint, its orange crust
Giving to deadly, perforated red.
Vague flowering bushes fuzz behind the shed
Foreground is a dogwood flowering
Whiter than the clouds, or anything.
Its shadows tangle on the outbuilding:
Gray on gray, flung like a Kline, they stripe
The complicated gesture of a tree,
At angles reproduce the waterpipe
Which drains the roof unnecessarily,
Casual on the manufactured wall.

Spring Morning, 1952

There is a mathematics in the air,
Another smell,
A new chill to the thawing mud
Under a dead-looking forsythia bush;
Logic is swollen with
The recurrent psychosis of the crocuses,
The square roots of ice,
The glittering fractions of morning.

The violence is a violence of scale
Shifting suddenly away from us
In triggered weather;
Bloom after bloom erupts
To release a vast
Fallout of pollen broadcast on the earth.
The planet which was put here for our use
Grows soluble and simple in our hands.

In this formula
Where the world works on paper,
When spring comes at last
Through a rough complex of muddy variables
From alphabetic shambles to new law,
You need not even look;
Once the math works,
The bomb will work.

Temporary Structure

I reflect on the buckling water
Of the cold creek
Where the present is thrown together.
The world shifts on its face, and flashes up
To move in the moment of a living mind
With all this trashy wild
Liquid and lunging forth.

I am makeshift;
Lean-to of body,
A few sticks of bone;
But my unfinished life
Is part of the world,
Part of the day
My eyes borrow.

It is a world
Of mud and meter and metal,
Stamped and seamed with sense,
A bright bucket tumbling in a creek
As my heart fills and empties, and my lungs
Give and take.
Unbroken, it is beaten back and forth

New, a booming shape
Banged and battered,
Its drum curve
Beaten by water,
Its flattened crystals blazing
Jammed between rocks,
One side in silver shadow.

Possibility
Rings in present air
With resounding sense,
But rings
Like the bucket turning over in the rocks:
Turned and overturned,
Bright zinc will wear off,

The bottom pock with rust,
Each pock
Enlarge with ruin, and,
Worn to a wafer,
The whole, punctured crust
Finally crumple under a loop
Of new water into a whorl of flakes.

What theory can contain
A muddy-metaled day
Cast from a wordless world and overturned
And turned along the rush and turbulence
Of nervous surfaces,
The cold, pictured flow
Charged with a constant change?

A theory balances,
But has to move
Unstable in a moving medium
Which can resist its equilibrium:
Clatter of day,
Sky thrown to the ground,
Light leaping up the trees.

A sounding mind
Can bang a tone of joy
Out of the bucket bouncing on the rocks,
The cold change of pebbles underwater,
Or a vessel sinking,
Clogged with bitter leaves,
And settling muffled to the hidden ooze.

This physical moment,
Circumstance of sense,
Is the living memory of having lived;
A rattling vision, thrown up from this bed,
The luscious frictions of another skin
Reshape the gathered day, and scatter out
A now of nerves and words.

Where the present is given up
Off balance
And poised between
Dangers of standing still
And risks of moving,
Running improvisation undermines
Imagined futures;

Being is being in momentum in
The unfinished business everywhere
Of verb and reverberation, galvanized
In a world of many movements
To shock-bright transitive sustained in sense;
Now is an echoing
Like the hollow of the bucket hammered on.

This living framework,
Scaffold for a life,
Will plunge into a cold scattering
Of its own accord,
Or at the world's will:
The scaffolding of my language taken down
Leave an emptiness of objects.

While I can stand,
Off-balance but alive
To punctuating rocks,
The run-on sky,
Dangling weeds and snarled clause of trees
That make the long sentence of the creek
Mean what it means,

This is the place to stand,
And let reflection fall
Unsafe in the crash of futures
And ongoing trade of surfaces and depths
Overturned and turned and turned again,
From which no thing escapes or is exempt:
This theory will also be a life.

The Way Out of the Wood

I

So I walked the brittle path crackling with glass
    And scattered twigs
Until right of way dissolved and I was stopped
    By boundary
Of barbed wire engrossed in thickets:
    Mud in thaw

Giving up its scrap iron.
    I turned
And followed the fence a long way down the hill.
    No path,
But tilts of embedded shale unevenly
    Led me down

Surfaces clumped with one-colored leaves
    Loose dirt
And other rock; no clear way
    But over logs
Propped and rotten in a tangle of dormant vine
    I went

Through thorny shadows sprawled and looped on rock
    My hand could break,
Steadied from tree to tree down the shale track
    In a long slant
Almost to the edge of a narrow creek
    At the bottom.

This was an unfamiliar gap in the wood:
    Dry vines
Knotted to the cleats of trees,
    Dead brush
In shade the color of a railroad spike,
    And my own absence

Cast ahead which had to mean
        Presence here—
Since, having wandered far from feeling
        Any certainty, I had come
Away from the roads I knew, following
        For a long time

The stubble ground under powerlines
        Which dipped and rose
On towering cages, iron armatures,
        Across cool fields,
Over and under slopes, disregarding property
        And highway,

Until, leaving the hum and crackle
        Of high-tension wires,
I followed an old path into these woods,
        Such as they were,
And like a drifting boat run suddenly aground,
        Came here.

Standing on a stump before the tangled water
        I looked back
Through February stalled before spring:
        Budless trees
Bare, dryrotted things, and the whole wood
        Relapsed into autumn

With the smell of rot released from frozen leaves:
        A false thaw
Raising the wreckage of memory
        From other seasons,
Preventing the simple momentum of the steps
        Which took me forward.

I turned again. The obstructed creek
        Glinted up,
Sun buckling on the water out of shape
        Through splintered limbs
And a snare of thorn; then
        Grappling

Through almost a break in growth I came to a flat
        Clear place
Where curving water
        Flickered
Out of the fallen woods.
        Bright seconds

Of creek shifted between transparent, thin
        Panels of ice
About to wash away: its light burden
        Of reflections carried
In downward treetops over irreducible
        Yellow pebbles

Some version of myself,
        Foreshortened, flat,
Wavering in and out of a shallow focus
        Over the paint-can
With its bottom rusted out, and Clorox bottle
        Split and white,

Full of mud and pebbles, but otherwise
        Indestructible,
Shuddering with everything in the creek's
        Continual drag
Of twigs and leaves and pebbles
        Along the bottom.

Caught between rocks downstream,
    A doubled branch
Loosened and shifted, untangling in sky,
    And unsnarled in me,
Through my scattered shadow, shifting with the rest
    On the quick

Shallow surface. I stood still on the bank.
    When the light
Changed suddenly
    I felt
The cold of clay ooze upward through my legs,
    Trees darken on my neck, and I saw

Into the involved heart of metal
    And fallen limbs
Where leaves were clumped and caught, until my mind
    Was water
But burdened with by-products,
    Choked with sediment,

Alive and moving, but imperfectly
    Fluid over gravel and glass,
And cluttered with commerce
    Come to its last shape
In the moving cold.
    I saw only

Things I had come so far
    To avoid awhile,
To walk and think
    In other terms
Than those assumed for me,
    Had followed me here.

I made an abscess where the wilderness
	Fell away.
The water in the creek slowed and stopped
	As, mixing in loose mud,
I looked into the ground glass of creek silt
	And sank

Almost to another time   when reason whirred from me
	Like a coin flung
Into a trash of vines and dormant things,
	And I stood
At the edge of a great machinery
	Disengaged.

Everything that moves delights in change,
	But I
Was hung on another time like a snagged branch
	Struggling to be water,
Flailing in eloquent shape from side to side
	But never forward.

Then the world leaked into me:
	First
Sense through punctures and pores,
	The cables clamped
To old ironwork of trees.
	Then

I shook from my own shudder of surfaces
	And heard the sound
Of the narrow water, moving as before
	Between where I was
And had to go; I balanced at the edge,
	And crossed the creek.

II

This side was briarless and cold, out of sun
    Most of the time, it seemed,
With fewer trees—tall sycamores
    Still hung with burrs,
And a few oaks and maples. Fallen things
    Scattered upward

Where the hillside rose ahead in its own shade
    To the fenceline,
Which, climbing almost to the ridge, disappeared
    In another thicket.
I met no stranger walking in that wood,
    No animals,

Only the trash and rocks
    Giving no guidance
Over landslides of shale and broken limbs
    Where I had to take myself;
But I climbed uphill easily, making a path
    To where the barbed-wire

Fence strung with brambles changed
    Its direction,
And the massed vines turned away with it.
    Downhill,
A glint of railbed showed between the limbs
    And empty shrubs,

And I made for its obvious track out of the wood,
    Although the slope down
Was lost in undergrowth and toppled trees.
    I climbed
Almost into the sun and moved downhill,
    Wading through

Uprooted stumps, gullies and barren spots
	Eroding under vines,
Over a world that scavenged on itself,
	Maple bones
Leaning deep into the light mattress of vines
	The color of iron,

And fallen sycamores overgrown, dismantled.
	Coming out of the cold
Leaning umber of the woods,
	My own shadow led me
Down between the standing sycamores
	To a frozen ditch,

Its red mud glittering with fishscale ice
	Too thawed to walk on,
Where the railbed rose up in a gravemound hump
	From bitter leaves
Half-liquid in red thaw. I jumped across,
	And scrambled

III

Up gravel and broken glass to level track.
    I followed the rails
Toward a curve which changed a little
    As I moved,
Its bed always glittering
    With glass

Found broken in dirty gravel between the ties
    But glittering on ahead
Where the woods were a dead sprawl of dormant growth.
    A month from here,
After the hard thaw, there would be
    Abundant drainage

Through clouds and leaves, a billion capillaries,
    Though now nothing was left
But skin and bones of tattered sycamores,
    And sky
Nailed to naked branches overhead
    With iron burrs.

Still the harsh wood oppressed me,
    Bitter with rot;
Monotonously plodding into it
    Over the level ties, as its air
Numbed me to the cold of minerals,
    I walked

An hour along the track
    Without seeing a house,
Crossroads, or human life:
    Only the wood,
Barren and open like a dismantled motor,
    Its parts strewn

Along the banks of the track. This narrow way
        Could only lead me
Through long corridors of landscape stained
        The color of transit,
Past backyards dark with sticky residue
        Of past combustion, on

To mammoth linkages, a great circuit
        Joining
In old ritual of conveyance
        Industrial parts
Of some great, sectioned city
        With the same

Rotten concrete and fences gone to rust,
        Corrugated streets,
Slag of peeling advertisements
        In blocks abandoned to
A holocaust of automobiles; and lives
        Lived or not lived

In terms of the marketplace. I heard the creek
        Ahead and under,
Where the railroad bridge
        Crossed a broad ditch;
My shadow turned, the gravel dropped away,
        And the woods opened.

IV

I walked unbraced onto the heavy framework
        Of the trestle,
Which crossed a gully where the creek
        I'd passed before
Curved into my path again. As I moved
        Its currents flashed

And flared up from gaps in structure
        Under me; sun-shocked
And fluent in the clear and present air,
        I felt
No more heaviness
        But only balanced

Over the good, cold creek cleaning its bed
        Of mattress-springs,
Bottle-glass and ice. Cool from the open
        Spaces between ties
Rushed around me as I stepped
        And sun was in my eyes

Warm and cold at once, the winter sun,
        Rush of things
Glossy and still in melt and movement,
        Over forgotten
Burdens of other times
        Remembered here

Only the way the creek
        Beneath me
Remembered the broken jars and mattress-springs
        Wedged between its rocks
As currents formed along them,
        Solvent water

Pouring through and around the junk,
    Wearing away
Long histories of use,
    Forgiving each thing of itself
Particle by particle, in its business
    Of always emptying.

I was absolved as well, in sun and wind,
    Winter again
A moment over rushing water
    And good cold
Cleansing thought: the sun's wafer
    Washed on the water surface

As if it would wear away, be borne away,
    But its idea kept
Firm in all that wobbling
    Of surfaces
Within elliptic shapes and scatterings
    Of flickered sparks

Across the stream, never held purely true,
    Tormented at times
By quick shakings, humps and shifts in current,
    But always accounting
Its shape, allowing circumstance;
    It crowned the stream.

But I crossed over; shadowy woods and weeds
    Surrounded me again
In their brown light, muffling the wash
    Of the creek
Until all I heard was my own step, plodding
    On dirt

Heavy timber and cracked rock
    Back
Into the muddy hardness of the wood
    Complicated in swamp
Thorn, vines and trash of trees
      To either side.

V

Another mile into the afternoon
    I stopped; to the side,
Bleak spaces between trees,
    Bone-colored ice,
A mess of leaves and deadfall
    Everywhere

Silence, excepting, when I moved, my step.
    I was tiring.
The stained line of ties spread far ahead
    Into endless trees
And silences with no more sign of life.
    Thinking I was alone,

The only one who might have come this way,
    I moved on, but my eye
Faltered over a foundation in the woods.
    Almost hidden there,
A house leaned heavily into its shadow's
    Abandoned shape,

Ransacked of its history.
    Whatever was left
In the warped roof and twist
    Of old structure
Straining toward collapse
    But lacking force,

Stood with another life among the wood's
    Natural wreckage,
Its frames forced out of shape,
    Its muddy glass
Reflecting all the undigested things
    Thawed loose

In this wrong weather. Suddenly the wood
    Was full of ghosts
Suspended in confusion between the seasons,
    And all the unrepaired,
Sunken, forgotten life
    Was rising up:

Shadows fell and ran in all directions
    From empty spots
In remembered light, flashing loose from leaves
    As a banged scar
Resurfaces to pulse original pain;
    In that confusion

Lives superimposed on things
    and things on lives
Rose in the empty wood and almost shimmered
    To solid life again,
In the lumbering shadows cast by trees long
    Fallen and gone.

Then the fires faded, and my tired eyes
    Looked down the track.
Over the crunch and dazzle of the glass and ice
    Toward horizon
Found underfoot, glazing a scum of grease
    Between ties

But glittering ahead
    Where I was going,
I walked, longing for space, to see the strip
    Of sky
High over the rails
    Opened again,

And closed in only by my curving eye.
    Shadows reached
Miles from the tops of trees'
    Intricacies
And rooted in my shadow as I walked:
    Brightness

Of high dusk burned in the comb of a hilltop,
    Golden
Over the sprawl of stones and sticks, beginning now
    The gradual
Abandonment of shapes
    Known again at dawn

When, if the thaw could end, and all the times
    The mud had given up
Sink back and harden to a winter air,
    Beside the twisted roof
Mud would digest the glass
    Sky decorated once.

Shadows were loosening their knots of debt
    Already, and I knew
Before color failed and fluttered on the last
    High
Tips of twigs where great sycamores reached
    Out of their shades,

I ought to find a way out of the wood, even if
    Only back to the place
I came from. Around another curve
    I saw
A dark circle in the railroad ditch
    To one side:

A tire in the weeds, full of water
    Iridescent, stagnant,
And half-sunk in muck,
    Tilted to point
Away where it might have come from through the brush,
    Rolling there

After a spirited abandonment,
    Bounced from a road
Somewhere nearby, which would be sure to lead
    Out to other roads,
Out of the woods, out of the afternoon
    Turning cold and dull.

VI

Where the woods thinned out into brackish thaw
    I followed my shadow down
The built embankment
    Onto the track
I myself made back into the trees,
    Wading into weeds

And gathering burrs, but soon finding a way
    Less overgrown
Through a stand of wild
    Honeylocust
That showed the sky through spines
    And flat, twisted pods,

Where I could make my path straight out
    Of the muddy wood
And wasted afternoon
    To built ground again.
I came through those trees
    A little uphill,

Where the earth was flat and solid, tilted, nude
    Of undergrowth:
Horse chestnuts, rotten acorns, and walnuts,
    Tennis-ball
Sized, the spongy bitter green
    Rotted away

From black interior, which stained my palm
    As I winged one ahead
And saw, up the gradual hill where it skipped to rest,
    The narrow mark
Of a gray strip between the thinning trees,
    Either fence

Or secondary road. Wiping my hand,
    I walked
Under the decorated sycamores,
    Bone white,
Hung with round burrs
    Like ornaments,

And came at last to the outskirts of the wood.
    Where my shadow turned
Down a pathless hillside covered with shrubs and trash,
    I picked my way among
The fallen trunks and branches of great trees,
    At times

Wading through leafmeal. At the edge,
    Enormous horizontals
Blazed through the line of oaks
    Marking the end of the wood;
Reddish-brown beyond a vine-bound fence,
    Middle dusk

Was iron oxide on an iron sky
    Over lanes of weeds
And a broad field of shapes glittering
    Through shrubs
Watered with gasoline,
    All going brilliant

Burnt-orange through an opening in the boundary.
    I found my way
Down through thorns a dry gray hillside, into
    A ditch
Clogged with acorn shells, and up along
    The fence

I held to, feeling its pattern
    Cold in my grip,
To steady my pace over piles of rotten leaves
    Toward the opening
Where I could walk under whole sky, away
    From the afternoon

And all the cluttered wood
    Had given up.
Through the chainlink, clogged with scrub,
    I could see
A lower level, of weeds laid out with paths;
    Reflecting shapes

Flashed like water in the strained sun.
    A fallen part of the fence
Opened downward, toward a gigantic wheel
    Of great, annihilated iron things
Scattered far and wide on a dirt lot.
    Walking into the last sun

VII

I crossed
Where chainlink fence, puckered and collapsing,
　　Tackled by undergrowth,
Was beaten down into the mud; and stood
　　At the edge of a junkyard.
Paths ran far ahead between stacks of cars

　　And piles of tires; roads
Spread toward the hub of the field like a city plan.
　　I passed,
Wading out of undergrowth, first
　　Onto a wide skirt
Of junk beyond the boundary of the yard,

　　Outside commerce,
Sold for the last time; there, in a waste of parts
　　Too scattered for salvaging,
Whole cars straddled the property line,
　　Their hoods gone, and leaned
Into new shapes across the thawing ground

　　With bloated magazines, split cassettes,
Magnetic tape unspooled, creased, stripped
　　Of information, inks long ago
Bled to one color as discarded ledgers
　　Swelled and buckled
And all ownership was given back

　　To materials
Resuming their own life in the open mud.
　　Just beyond
Where the woods petered out, and just before
　　The junkyard boundary,
I had come at last to the end of the marketplace.

I walked the unmarked ground
Looking for some path in the high grass
  To lead me across the margin,
In among the tenement stacks of cars
  And on into
The great wealth of our waste,

  Here was everything
Marked down to nothing,
  And supply
Scattered out of stock,
  Beyond demand,
Entering the economy of snails.

  As I passed through
That rind between places, where anything
  Could fall unclaimed,
Forgotten except by weather
 · Between untended properties,
The junkyard rose ahead through littered weeds,

  And saw
My poor present refracted through the glass
  Of other times,
To other purposes:
  I thought I saw
A shattered windshield glinting whole again,

  Its hanging glass
Fill with a morning sky; and then I saw
  Things first
Give up their histories to noon light
  Then afternoon
Until at last, here by the fence of trees

Darkening
In the oldest languages
    Of rust and glitter,
All things gave up their history
    To now.
Dusk followed me

    Coming out of the cool
Woods onto the broadness of the lot,
    Where I found
Long, geometric aisles in the high grass
    And littered mud,
Crackling with each step the dark ground's

    Literal glitter
Of jars and headlights, safety glass and mirrors
    Between cars, each
Preserving the after-instant
    Of its wreck
In cold shape of reaction.

VIII

I entered the yard,
Where bodies of automobiles, piled up high,
   Made a maze
In which I wandered always inward,
   On layers of glass and trash,
Through dark corridors of mineral

   For a long time
I followed what I found to follow there,
   From sky to fractured sky,
Through inventory of old accidents,
   Across a field
Glittering with the sense of other lives

   Remembered
Only in what was wasted
   And reduced
To harden to this crust of time and place.
   Broken down,
Unburdened in this field, multiplied

   Past any value,
Only these stubborn husks remained of lives
   Lived out in work
Without hope of infamy or praise,
   Spent for money
And exhausted here.

   Rounding
In the long circles of concentric paths
   Overtaken machinery
Unadvertised, unbargained for,
   Brought here
After what danger, labor, sacrifice,

I found
The purpose of the road,
   A cleared space
All paths converged upon, and ended in,
   At the hub of the yard.
I stood at the center, and looked out from there

   At the heavy pattern
Laid down enormously across the field:
   I had come across
A neglected place, far from busy lives,
   Where all our evidence
Lay uncovered in a winter thaw—

   Our history held up
An instant in a windshield's glittering, limp
   Concavity,
Then drained into its dark record of impact:
   Cause known only
In rough configuration of effect.

   The spot,
Windless and quiet, where I stood,
   Was the eye
Of our terrible hurricane;
   I had found
The secret center of America.

   Everywhere I looked
To follow the scheme imposed across the field
   I could see
Elements of obliterated lives
   Consumed
And totaled in the process of this place;

And I saw that more
Was never wasted, than the vast
        Anti-economy
Expanding from this point—
        Or never wasted long.
This was no desolation from a bomb.

        We built this city.
Our machinery made this, and demanded
        Daily fuel
Of human work and life,
        Involving us
To raise its product higher.

        Following
My shadow changing where it ran ahead
        Over changed things,
I headed through a vacancy outspread
        Over the great field,
Away from the stacks of cars

        Toward what must be
Other boundaries of fence and road,
        Laid to rust
On outskirts of outskirts, this place where all roads
        Dead-ended in high grass.
Leaving the center of the yard, I saw

        Slow darkening
Making the field of things its other self,
        As air rusted through
To show the spaces underneath the hood,
        The dark gap
Around the engine.

IX

The cold returned,
Resounding winter;
    Cracks crawled
On knocked windshields wrestling with their shapes,
    And contracting metal
Sounded in all the circles outlying

    As a February air
Rose from the railbeds in a billion crystals
    Over paths
Littered with glass needles,
    Where the quick continual
Had hovered all morning on the outstripped metal.

    Now,
Passing the highest, hollow stacks of cars,
    Having made my way
Through the cold rummage of the thawing wood
    Only to a clearing
At the center of a junkyard, I came

    Out among
The last shapes of cars
    Pried apart
At hinge and weld with the slow, insinuated crow-
    Bar of a tree's shadow,
And finding a likely road, followed it

    Outward into
The dazzle going dead
    Throughout the field,
Like the wobbling-down
    After a wreck
Of a loose hubcap rolled along the pavement.

—Only
The stalled world
        Turning
Again on its axis,
        And the air
Whitening in my exhausted breath

        As the whole sky drained
Through the black zero chipped into a windshield.
        Having walked
All day through the roadless wood to find this lot
        Full of roads,
Honeycombed with roads, at the end of roads,

        I followed another road
Where even dusk had stalled, moving again
        Past iron-flecked
Bowls of upturned hubcaps filled with water,
        Cold and tired,
Carrying nothing with me out of there.

X

I made my way
Toward a battered gate ajar
    In the last light;
My shadow, dying out, streaked far ahead
    Into the planet's shadow,
And rambled over gravel to the gate.

    The shale-colored sky
Was losing its last layered sediment
    To settled dark
Where, such as it was, the usual world
    Stretched out
In little better order than the yard,

    An area of lights
Brightening with the present and the cold.
    I felt
February tauten in the rigid metals
    Contracting more:
It was the end of autumn. Branches snapped

    In the sound of my shoes on glass,
And I left the rot and tangle of the wood
    Far behind
As starry points of sycamore burrs
    Were buried
In the smoke of the cold sky darkening.

The gravel path
Led outward to all roads beyond the fence
Marking off
The boundary of the dead afternoon. Ahead,
All paths
Are glittering with glass as I walk out.

New York, 1985–1988